PRAYERS AND PROMISES FOR

Women

A Topical Devotional

PRAYERS AND PROMISES FOR

Women

The quoted ideas expressed in this book (but not scripture verses) are not, in all cases, exact quotations, as some have been edited for clarity and brevity. In all cases, the author has attempted to maintain the speaker's original intent. In some cases, quoted material for this book was obtained from secondary sources, primarily print media. While every effort was made to ensure the accuracy of these sources, the accuracy cannot be guaranteed. For additions, deletions, corrections or clarifications in future editions of this text, please write BRIGHTON BOOKS.

Printed in the United States of America
Cover Design: Holli Conger
Page Layout: Bart Dawson

1 2 3 4 5 6 7 8 9 10 • 03 04 05 06 07 08 09 10

Table of Contents

Introduction

*B*eing a godly woman in today's world can be a daunting task. Never have expectations been higher, never have temptations been so plentiful, and never have demands been greater…and that's where God comes in. God stands ready, willing, and able to help us in every facet of our lives *if* we ask Him. But it's important to remember that the best way to ask God for His wisdom and His strength is to ask Him *often*.

Sometimes, when it seems that we have too many things to do and too few hours in which to do them, we may be tempted to rush through the day with little or no time for prayer and meditation; when we do so, we suffer because of our mistaken priorities. But, when we set aside time each day for God, we open ourselves to His love, His wisdom, and His strength.

The fabric of daily life is woven together with the threads of habit, and no habit is more important than that of consistent prayer and daily devotion to our Creator. This text contains a collection of brief devotional readings arranged by topic. Each two-page chapter contains Bible verses, a devotional reading, quotations from noted Christian thinkers, and a prayer.

This text addresses topics of particular interest to you, a Christian woman living in an uncertain world. If you take the time to meditate upon these devotional readings, you will be reminded of God's love, of His Son, and of His promises. May these pages be a blessing to you, and may you, in turn, be a blessing to those whom God has seen fit to place along your path.

The Abundant Life

I am come that they might have life, and
that they might have it more abundantly.
John 10:10 KJV

God does not promise us abundance. He
promises that we "might have life" and that we
"might have it more abundantly" if we accept His
grace, His blessings, and His Son. When we commit
our hearts and our days to the One who created us,
we experience spiritual abundance through the grace
and sacrifice of His Son, Jesus. But, when we focus
our thoughts and energies not upon God's perfect
will for our lives but instead upon our own unending
assortments of earthly needs and desires, we
inevitably forfeit the spiritual abundance that might
otherwise be ours.

Today and every day, seek God's will for your
life and follow it. Today, turn your worries and your
concerns over to your Heavenly Father. Today, seek
God's wisdom, follow His commandments, trust His
judgment, and honor His Son. When you do,
spiritual abundance will be yours, not just for this
day but for all eternity.

If we were given all we wanted here, our hearts
would settle for this world rather than the next.

Elisabeth Elliot

Get ready for God to show you not only
His pleasure, but His approval.

Joni Eareckson Tada

And God is able to make all grace abound to you,
so that always having all sufficiency in everything,
you may have an abundance for every good deed.

2 Corinthians 9:8 NASB

Dear Lord, I praise You for the abundant life that
is mine through Christ Jesus. Guide me according
to Your will, and help me to be a worthy servant
in all that I say and do. Give me courage, Lord,
to claim the rewards You have promised, and
when I do, let the glory be Yours.

~Amen

Accepting Christ

It is a trustworthy statement, deserving
full acceptance, that Christ Jesus
came into the world to save sinners....

1 Timothy 1:15 NASB

God's love for you is deeper and more profound than you can imagine. God's love for you is so great that He sent His only Son to this earth to die for your sins and to offer you the priceless gift of eternal life. Now, you must decide whether or not to accept God's gift. Will you ignore it or embrace it? Will you return it or neglect it? Will you accept Christ, or will you turn from Him?

Your decision to accept Christ is the pivotal decision of your life. It is a decision that you cannot ignore. It is a decision that is yours and yours alone. It is a decision with profound consequences, both earthly and eternal. Accept God's gift: accept Christ today.

The redemption, accomplished for us by
our Lord Jesus Christ on the cross at Calvary,
is redemption from the power of sin as well as
from its guilt. Christ is able to save all
who come unto God by Him.

Hannah Whitall Smith

Thoughts on the Transforming Power of Christ

The amazing thing about Jesus is that He doesn't just patch up our lives, He gives us a brand new sheet, a clean slate to start over, all new.

Gloria Gaither

I have a great need for Christ;
I have a great Christ for my need.

C. H. Spurgeon

I am able to do all things through Him
who strengthens me.

Philippians 4:13 HCSB

Dear Lord, You sent Your Son to this earth that we might have the gift of eternal life. Thank You, Father, for that priceless gift. Help me to share the wondrous message of Jesus with others so that they, too, might accept Him as their Savior. And, let me praise You always for the new life You have given me, a life that is both abundant and eternal.

~Amen

Anxiety

Do not be anxious about anything, but in everything, by prayer and petition, with thanksgiving,
present your requests to God.

Philippians 4:6 NIV

We live in a world that sometimes seems to
shift beneath our feet. From time to time, all of us
face adversity, discouragement, or disappointment.
And, throughout life, we must all endure life-
changing personal losses that leave us breathless.
When we do, God stands ready to protect us.
Psalm 147 promises, "He heals the brokenhearted,
and binds their wounds" (v. 3, NIV). When we are
troubled, we must call upon God, and, in His own
time and according to His own plan, He will heal us.

Are you anxious? Take those anxieties to God.
Are you troubled? Take your troubles to Him. Does
your world seem to be trembling beneath your feet?
Seek protection from the One who cannot be moved.
The same God who created the universe will protect
you if you ask Him...so ask Him.

Look around you and you'll be distressed;
look within yourself and you'll be depressed;
look at Jesus, and you'll be at rest!

Corrie ten Boom

Thoughts on God's Comfort

The moment anxious thoughts invade your mind,
go to the Lord in prayer. Look first to God.
Then, you will see the cause of your anxiety
in a whole new light.

Kay Arthur

The beginning of anxiety is the end of faith, and
the beginning of true faith is the end of anxiety.

George Mueller

But God, who comforts the humble,
comforted us . . . .

2 Corinthians 7:6 HCSB

Dear Lord, sometimes troubles and distractions
preoccupy thoughts and trouble my soul.
When I am anxious, let me turn my prayers to
You. When I am worried, give me faith in You.
Let me live courageously, Dear God, knowing that
You love me and that You will protect me,
today and forever.

~Amen

Asking God

Ask and it will be given to you; seek and you will
find; knock and the door will be opened to you.
For everyone who asks receives;
he who seeks finds; and to him who knocks,
the door will be opened.

Matthew 7:7-8 NIV

Sometimes, amid the demands and the
frustrations of everyday life, we forget to slow
ourselves down long enough to talk with God.
Instead of turning our thoughts and prayers to Him,
we rely instead upon our own resources. Instead of
praying for strength and courage, we seek to
manufacture it within ourselves. Instead of asking
God for guidance, we depend only upon our own
limited wisdom. The results of such behaviors are
unfortunate and, on occasion, tragic.

Are you in need? Ask God to sustain you. Are
you troubled? Take your worries to Him in prayer.
Are you weary? Seek God's strength. In all things
great and small, seek God's wisdom and His grace.
He hears your prayers, and He will answer. All you
must do is ask.

God will help us become the people
we are meant to be, if only we will ask Him.

Hannah Whitall Smith

Petitioning God

God makes prayer as easy as possible for us.
He's completely approachable and available, and
He'll never mock or upbraid us for bringing
our needs before Him.

Shirley Dobson

When trials come your way—as inevitably
they will—do not run away.
Run to your God and Father.

Kay Arthur

So I say to you, keep asking, and it will be given
to you. Keep searching, and you will find. Keep
knocking, and the door will be opened to you.

Luke 11:9 HCSB

Lord, You are the Giver of all things good.
When I am in need, let me come to You in prayer.
You know the desires of my heart, Lord;
grant them, I ask. Yet not my will, Father,
but Your will be done.

~Amen

Attitude

Whatever is true, whatever is noble, whatever
is right, whatever is pure, whatever is lovely,
whatever is admirable—if anything is excellent or
praiseworthy—think about such things.

Philippians 4:8 NIV

As Christian women, we have every reason
to rejoice. God is in His heaven; Christ has risen,
and we are the sheep of His flock. But, when the
demands of life seem great and our resources seem
small by comparison, we may find ourselves
exhausted or discouraged, or both.

What's your attitude today? Are you fearful,
angry, or worried? Are you confused, bitter, or
pessimistic? If so, God wants to have a little chat
with you.

God created you in His own image, and He wants
you to experience His joy and abundance. But, God
will not force His joy upon you; you must claim it for
yourself. So today, and every day hereafter, celebrate
this life that God has given you. Think optimistically
about yourself and your future. Give thanks to the
One who has given you everything, and trust in your
heart that He wants to give you so much more.

The Importance of Our Thoughts

The things we think are the things that feed our
souls. If we think on pure and lovely things,
we shall grow pure and lovely like them;
and the converse is equally true.

Hannah Whitall Smith

I could go through this day oblivious to
the miracles all around me, or
I could tune in and "enjoy."

Gloria Gaither

Set your mind on the things above,
not on the things that are on earth.

Colossians 3:2 NASB

Lord, I pray for an attitude that is Christlike.
Whatever the circumstances I face, whether
good or bad, triumphal or tragic, may my response
reflect a God-honoring, Christlike attitude
of optimism, faith, and love for You.

~Amen

Celebration

Shout for joy to the LORD, all the earth.
Worship the LORD with gladness;
come before him with joyful songs.

Psalm 100:1-2 NIV

The 100th Psalm reminds us that the entire earth should "Shout for joy to the Lord." As God's children, we are blessed beyond measure, but sometimes, as busy women living in a demanding world, we are slow to count our gifts and even slower to give thanks to the Giver.

Our blessings include life and health, family and friends, freedom and possessions—for starters. And, the gifts we receive from God are multiplied when we share them. May we always give thanks to God for His blessings, and may we always demonstrate our gratitude by sharing our gifts with others.

The 118th Psalm reminds us that, "This is the day which the LORD has made; let us rejoice and be glad in it" (v. 24 NASB). May we celebrate this day and the One who created it.

Praise Him! Praise Him!
Tell of His excellent greatness;
Praise Him! Praise Him! Ever in joyful song.

Fanny Crosby

Celebrating God's Glorious Gifts

The Bible instructs—and experience teaches—
that praising God results in our burdens being
lifted and our joys being multiplied.

Mary Prince

When an honest soul can get still before the living
Christ, we can still hear Him say simply and
clearly, "Love the Lord your God with all your
heart and with all your soul and with all your
mind…and love one another as I have loved you."

Gloria Gaither

Rejoice in the Lord always.
I will say it again: Rejoice!

Philippians 4:4 HCSB

Lord God, the heavens proclaim Your handiwork,
and every star in the sky tells of Your power. You
sent Your Son to die for my sins, and You gave me
the gift of eternal life. Let me be mindful of all my
blessings, and let me celebrate You and Your
marvelous creation. Today is Your gift to me, Lord.
Let me use it to Your glory.

~Amen

Cheerfulness

The cheerful heart has a continual feast.

Proverbs 15:15 NIV

Few things in life are more sad, or, for that matter, more absurd, than a grumpy Christian. Christ promises us lives of abundance and joy, but He does not impose His joy upon us. We must claim His joy for ourselves, and when we do, Jesus, in turn, fills our spirits with His power and His love.

How can we receive from Christ the joy that is rightfully ours? By giving Him what is rightfully His: our hearts and our souls.

When we earnestly commit ourselves to the Savior of mankind, when we place Jesus at the center of our lives and trust Him as our personal Savior, He will transform us, not just for today, but for all eternity. Then we, as God's children, can share Christ's joy and His message with a world that needs both.

Our obedience does not make God any bigger
or better than He already is. Anything God
commands of us is so that our joy may be full—
the joy of seeing His glory revealed to us and in us!

Beth Moore

Preoccupy my thoughts with your praise
beginning today.
Joni Eareckson Tada

It is not how much we have, but how much
we enjoy, that makes our happiness.
C. H. Spurgeon

Happy is he...whose hope is in
the LORD his God.
Psalm 146:5 KJV

Dear Lord, You have given me so many reasons
to celebrate. Today, let me choose an attitude
of cheerfulness. Let me be a joyful Christian,
Lord, quick to laugh and slow to anger.
Let me praise You, Lord, and give thanks for
our blessings. Today is Your creation;
let me celebrate it...and You.
~Amen

Children

And he took a child, and set him in the midst
of them: and when he had taken him in his arms,
he said unto them, whosoever shall receive one
of such children in my name, receiveth me; and
whosoever shall receive me, receiveth not me,
but him that sent me.

Mark 9:36-37 KJV

Every child is a priceless gift from the Creator.
And, with the Father's gift comes immense
responsibility. As parents, friends of parents, aunts,
and grandmothers, we understand the critical
importance of raising our children with love, with
discipline, and with God.

As Christians, we are commanded to care for
our children . . . all of them. Let us care for our
children here at home and pray for all children
around the world. Every child is God's child. May
we, as concerned adults, behave—and pray—
accordingly.

Our faithfulness, or lack of it, will have
an overwhelming impact on the heritage
of our children.

Beth Moore

Thoughts about Our Children

Children are not so different from kites.
Children were created to fly. But, they need wind,
the undergirding, and strength that comes from
unconditional love, encouragement, and prayer.

Gigi Graham Tchividjian

Children are the hands by which
we take hold of heaven.

Henry Ward Beecher

Let the little children come to Me;
don't stop them, for the kingdom
of God belongs to such as these.

Mark 10:14 HCSB

Lord, the children of this world are Your children.
Let us love them, care for them, nurture them,
teach them, and lead them to You. And today,
as I serve as an example to the children under my
care, let my words and deeds demonstrate the love
that I feel for them . . . and for You.

~Amen

Christ's Love

For I am persuaded, that neither death, nor life,
nor angels, nor principalities, nor powers, nor
things present, nor things to come, nor height,
nor depth, nor any other creature, shall be able
to separate us from the love of God,
which is in Christ Jesus our Lord.

Romans 8:38-39 KJV

What does the love of Christ mean to His believers? It changes everything. His love is perfect and steadfast. Even though we are fallible, and wayward, the Good Shepherd cares for us still. Even though we have fallen far short of the Father's commandments, Christ loves us with a power and depth that is beyond our understanding. And, as we accept Christ's love and walk in Christ's footsteps, our lives bear testimony to His power and to His grace.

Indeed, Christ's love changes everything; may we invite Him into our hearts so it can then change everything in us.

Jesus is all compassion. He never betrays us.

Catherine Marshall

The Love of Christ...

Keep your face upturned to Christ as
the flowers do to the sun. Look, and
your soul shall live and grow.
Hannah Whitall Smith

In your greatest weakness, turn to your greatest
strength, Jesus, and hear Him say, "My grace is
sufficient for you, for My strength is made perfect
in weakness" (2 Corinthians 12:9 NKJV).
Lisa Whelchel

We love him, because he first loved us.
1 John 4:19 KJV

Dear Jesus, I am humbled by Your love and mercy.
You went to Calvary so that I might have eternal
life. Thank You, Jesus, for Your priceless gift, and
for Your love. You loved me first, Lord, and
I will return Your love today and forever.
~Amen

The Church

Take heed therefore unto yourselves, and to all the flock, over the which the Holy Ghost hath made you overseers, to feed the church of God....

Acts 20:28 KJV

In the Book of Acts, Luke reminds us to "feed the church of God." As Christians who have been saved by a loving, compassionate Creator, we are compelled not only to worship Him in our hearts but also to worship Him in the presence of fellow believers.

The church belongs to God; it is His just as certainly as we are His. When we help build God's church, we bear witness to the changes that He has made in our lives.

Today and every day, let us worship God with grateful hearts and helping hands as we support the church that He has created. Let us witness to our friends, to our families, and to the world. When we do so, we bless others and we are blessed by the One who sent His Son to die so that we might have eternal life.

And how can we improve the church?
Simply and only by improving ourselves.

A. W. Tozer

Every time a new person comes to God, every time
someone's gifts find expression in the fellowship of
believers, every time a family in need is surrounded
by the caring church, the truth is affirmed anew:
the Church triumphant is alive and well!

Gloria Gaither

The church has no greater need today than
to fall in love with Jesus all over again.

Vance Havner

Now you are Christ's body, and
individually members of it.

1 Corinthians 12:27 NASB

Dear Lord, today I pray for Your church. Let me
help to feed Your flock by helping to build
Your church so that others, too, might experience
Your enduring love and Your eternal grace.

~Amen

Contentment

I have learned, in whatsoever state I am,
therewith to be content.

Philippians 4:11 KJV

The preoccupation with happiness and
contentment is an ever-present theme in the modern
world. We are bombarded with messages that tell us
where to find peace and pleasure in a world that
worships materialism and wealth. But, lasting
contentment is not found in material possessions;
genuine contentment is a spiritual gift from God to
those who trust in Him and follow His
commandments.

Where do we find contentment? If we don't find
it in God, we will never find it anywhere else. But, if
we put our faith and our trust in Him, we will be
blessed with an inner peace that is beyond human
understanding. When God dwells at the center of
our lives, peace and contentment will belong to us
just as surely as we belong to God.

Those who are God's without reserve are,
in every sense, content.

Hannah Whitall Smith

Contentment through Christ

Rejoicing is a matter of obedience to God—
an obedience that will start you on the road
to peace and contentment.

Kay Arthur

We might occasionally be able to change
our circumstances, but only God can
change our hearts.

Beth Moore

Let your character be free from the love of money,
being content with what you have;
for He Himself has said, "I will never desert you,
nor will I ever forsake you."

Hebrews 13:5 NASB

Dear Lord, You are my contentment and my peace.
I find protection when I seek Your healing hand; I
discover joy when I welcome Your healing Spirit.
Let me look to You, Lord, for the peace and
contentment that You have offered me through
the gift of Your Son.

~Amen

Difficult Days

In this world you will have trouble. But take heart!
I have overcome the world.

John 16:33 NIV

All of us face difficult days. Sometimes even
the most devout Christian women can become
discouraged, and you are no exception. After all, you
live in a world where expectations can be high and
demands can be even higher.

If you find yourself enduring difficult
circumstances, remember that God remains in His
heaven. If you become discouraged with the direction
of your day or your life, turn your thoughts and prayers
to Him. He is a God of possibility, not negativity.
He will guide you through your difficulties and
beyond them. And then, with a renewed spirit of
optimism and hope, you can thank the Giver of all
things good for gifts that are simply too numerous to
count.

Every misfortune, every failure, every loss may be
transformed. God has the power to transform all
misfortunes into "God-sends."

Mrs. Charles E. Cowman

Let's thank God for allowing us to experience
troubles that drive us closer to Him.

Shirley Dobson

Often the trials we mourn are really gateways
into the good things we long for.

Hannah Whitall Smith

He restoreth my soul: he leadeth me in the paths
of righteousness for his name's sake.

Psalm 23:3 KJV

Dear Heavenly Father, when I am troubled,
You heal me. When I am afraid, You protect me.
When I am discouraged, You lift me up. You are
my unending source of strength, Lord; let me turn
to You when I am weak. In the difficult days of my
life, let me trust Your plan and Your will. And
whatever my circumstances, Lord, let me always
give the thanks and the glory to You.

~Amen

Energy

I am able to do all things through Him
who strengthens me.

Philippians 4:13 HCSB

All of us have moments when we feel drained. All of us suffer through difficult days, trying times, and perplexing periods of our lives. Thankfully, God stands ready and willing to give us comfort and strength if we turn to Him.

Burning the candle at both ends is tempting but potentially destructive. Instead, we should place first things first by saying no to the things that we simply don't have the time or the energy to do. As we establish our priorities, we should turn to God and to His Holy Word for guidance.

If you're a woman with too many demands and too few hours in which to meet them, don't fret. Instead, focus upon God and upon His love for you. Then, ask Him for the wisdom to prioritize your life and the strength to fulfill your responsibilities. God will give you the energy to do the most important things on today's to-do list…if you ask Him. So ask Him.

Worry does not empty tomorrow of its sorrow;
it empties today of its strength.

Corrie ten Boom

Our Strength Comes from God

We are never stronger than the moment
we admit we are weak.

Beth Moore

Where there is much prayer, there will be much
of the Spirit; where there is much of the Spirit,
there will be ever-increasing power.

Andrew Murray

The LORD is the strength of my life.

Psalm 27:1 KJV

Lord, let me find my strength in You.
When I am weary, give me rest. When I feel
overwhelmed, let me look to You for my priorities.
Let Your power be my power, Lord, and let
Your way be my way, today and forever.

~Amen

Evil

Submit yourselves therefore to God. Resist the
devil, and he will flee from you. Draw nigh to
God, and he will draw nigh to you.

James 4:7-8 KJV

This world is God's creation, and it contains
the wonderful fruits of His handiwork. But, it also
contains countless opportunities to stray from God's
will. Temptations are everywhere, and the devil, it
seems, never takes a day off. Our task, as believers, is
to turn away from temptation and to place our lives
squarely in the center of God's will.

In a letter to believers, Peter offers a stern
warning: "Your adversary, the devil, prowls around
like a roaring lion, seeking someone to devour"
(I Peter 5:8 NASB). What was true in New
Testament times is equally true in our own. Satan
tempts his prey and then devours them. As believing
Christian women, we must beware. And, if we seek
righteous-ness in our own lives, we must earnestly
wrap ourselves in the protection of God's Holy Word.
When we do, we are secure.

As a child of God, you are no longer a slave to sin.

Kay Arthur

Resisting the Evils of the World

We are in a continual battle with the spiritual
forces of evil, but we will triumph when
we yield to God's leading and call on
His powerful presence in prayer.

Shirley Dobson

God shapes the world by prayer. The more praying
there is in the world, the better the world will be,
and the mightier will be the forces against evil.

E. M. Bounds

He shall not be afraid of evil tidings:
his heart is fixed, trusting in the LORD.

Psalm 112:7 KJV

Dear Lord, because You have given Your children
free will, the world is a place where evil threatens
our lives and our souls. Protect us, Father, from the
evils and temptations of this difficult age. Help us
to trust You, Father, and to obey Your Word,
knowing that Your ultimate victory over evil is
both inevitable and complete.

~Amen

But Jesus turned him about, and when he saw her,
he said, Daughter, be of good comfort; thy faith
hath made thee whole. And the woman
was made whole from that hour.

Matthew 9:22 KJV

Every life—including yours—is a series of successes and failures, celebrations and disappointments, joys and sorrows. Jesus taught his disciples that if they had faith, they could move mountains. You can too.

When a suffering woman sought healing by merely touching the hem of His cloak, Jesus replied, "Daughter, be of good comfort; thy faith hath made thee whole." The message to believers of every generation is clear: live by faith today and every day.

When you place your faith, your trust, indeed your life in the hands of Christ Jesus, you'll be amazed at the marvelous things He can do with you and through you. So strengthen your faith through praise, through worship, through Bible study, and through prayer. And trust God's plans. With Him, all things are possible, and He stands ready to open a world of possibilities to you . . . if you have faith.

The Power of Faith

Faith is a strong power, mastering any difficulty
in the strength of the Lord who made
heaven and earth.

Corrie ten Boom

Faith in faith is pointless. Faith in a living,
active God moves mountains.

Beth Moore

If ye have faith as a grain of mustard seed…
nothing shall be impossible unto you.

Matthew 17:20 KJV

Lord, sometimes this world is a terrifying place.
When I am filled with uncertainty and doubt,
give me faith. In life's dark moments, help me
remember that You are always near and that You
can overcome any challenge. Today, Lord, and
forever, I will place my trust in You.

~Amen

Family

These should learn first of all to put their religion
into practice by caring for their own family.
1 Timothy 5:4 NIV

In the life of every family, there are moments
of frustration and disappointment. Lots of them. But,
for those who are lucky enough to live in the presence
of a close-knit, caring clan, the rewards far outweigh
the frustrations.

No family is perfect, and neither is yours. But,
despite the inevitable challenges and hurt feelings
of family life, your clan is God's gift to you. That
little band of men, women, kids, and babies is a
priceless treasure on temporary loan from the Father
above. Give thanks to the Giver for the gift of
family...and act accordingly.

A home is a place where we find
direction and love.
Gigi Graham Tchividjian

Thoughts on Family Life

The family that prays together, stays together.
Anonymous

The secret of a happy home life is that
the members of the family learn to give
and receive love.
Billy Graham

Choose for yourselves this day whom
you will serve…as for me and my household,
we will serve the LORD.
Joshua 24:15 NIV

Dear Lord, I am blessed to be part of the family
of God where I find love and acceptance. You
have also blessed me with my earthly family.
Today, I pray for my family and for families
throughout our world. Protect us and guide us,
Lord. And, as I reach out to my own family,
may I show them the same love and care that
You have shown to me.
~Amen

Fear

For God hath not given us the spirit of fear; but
of power, and of love, and of a sound mind.

2 Timothy 1:7 KJV

Even the most dedicated Christian woman may
find her courage tested by the inevitable
disappointments and tragedies of life. After all, we
live in a dangerous world filled with uncertainty,
hardship, sickness, and danger. Old Man Trouble, it
seems, is never too far from the front door.

When we focus upon our fears and our doubts,
we may find many reasons to lie awake at night and
fret about the uncertainties of the coming day. A
better strategy, of course, is to focus not upon our
fears, but instead upon our God.

God is as near as your next breath, and He is in
control. He offers salvation to all His children,
including you. God is your shield and your strength;
you are His forever. So don't focus your thoughts upon
the fears of the day. Instead, trust God's plan and
His eternal love for you. And remember: whatever
the size of your challenge, God is bigger.

When once we are assured that God is good, then
there can be nothing left to fear.

Hannah Whitall Smith

In a Difficult World, We Must Trust God

Worry is a cycle of inefficient thoughts whirling
around a center of fear.

Corrie ten Boom

Are you fearful? First, bow your head and pray for
God's strength. Then, raise your head and look
Old Man Trouble squarely in the eye. Chances are,
Old Man Trouble will blink.

Mary Prince

Fear not: for I have redeemed thee, I have called
thee by thy name; thou art mine.

Isaiah 43:1 KJV

Heavenly Father, when I am fearful,
keep me mindful that You are my protector and
my salvation. Give me strength, Lord, to face
the challenges of this day as I gain
my courage from You.

~Amen

Forgiveness

And be ye kind one to another, tenderhearted,
forgiving one another, even as God
for Christ's sake hath forgiven you.

Ephesians 4:32 KJV

There's no doubt about it: forgiveness is difficult.
Being frail, fallible, imperfect human beings, we are
quick to anger, quick to blame, slow to forgive, and
even slower to forget. Yet as Christians, we are
commanded to forgive others, just as we, too, have
been forgiven. So even when forgiveness is difficult,
we must ask God to help us move beyond the spiritual
stumbling blocks of bitterness and hate.

If, in your heart, you hold bitterness against even
a single person, forgive. If there exists even one
person, alive or dead, whom you have not forgiven,
follow God's commandment and His will for your
life: forgive. If you are embittered against yourself
for some past mistake or shortcoming, forgive. Then,
to the best of your abilities, forget. And move on.
Bitterness and regret are not part of God's plan for
your life. Forgiveness is.

He who cannot forgive others breaks the bridge
over which he himself must pass.

Corrie ten Boom

The Spirit of Forgiveness

I believe that forgiveness can become a continuing
cycle: because God forgives us, we're to forgive
others; because we forgive others, God forgives us.
Scripture presents both parts of the cycle.

Shirley Dobson

Forgiveness is the precondition of love.

Catherine Marshall

Blessed are the merciful:
for they shall obtain mercy.

Matthew 5:7 KJV

Heavenly Father, forgiveness is Your
commandment, and I know that I should forgive
others just as You have forgiven me. But, genuine
forgiveness is difficult. Help me to forgive those
who have injured me, and deliver me from the
traps of anger and bitterness. Forgiveness is
Your way, Lord; let it be mine.

~Amen

A friend loves at all times, and a brother
is born for adversity.

Proverbs 17:17 NIV

What is a friend? The dictionary defines the word *friend* as "a person who is attached to another by feelings of affection or personal regard." This definition is accurate, as far as it goes, but when we examine the deeper meaning of friendship, so many more descriptors come to mind: trustworthiness, loyalty, helpfulness, kindness, understanding, forgiveness, encouragement, humor, and cheerfulness, to mention but a few.

Genuine friendship should be treasured and nourished. As Christians, we are governed by the Golden Rule: we are commanded to treat others as we wish to be treated. When we treat others with kindness, courtesy, and respect, we build friendships that can last a lifetime. And God smiles.

In friendship, God opens your eyes to
the glories of Himself.

Joni Eareckson Tada

Don't bypass the potential for meaningful
friendships just because of differences.
Explore them. Embrace them. Love them.
Luci Swindoll

Some people come into our lives and quickly go.
Some people stay for awhile and leave footprints
on our hearts, and we are never the same.
Anonymous

Thine own friend, and thy father's friend,
forsake not....
Proverbs 27:10 KJV

Lord, thank You for my friends. Let me be
a trustworthy friend to others, and let my love for
You be reflected in my genuine love for them.
~Amen

Generosity

Now this I say, he who sows sparingly will also reap sparingly, and he who sows bountifully will also reap bountifully. Each one must do just as he has purposed in his heart, not grudgingly or under compulsion, for God loves a cheerful giver.

2 Corinthians 9:6-7 NASB

The words of Jesus are clear: "Freely you have received, freely give" (Matthew 10:8 NIV). As followers of Christ, we are commanded to be generous with our friends, with our families, and with those in need. We must give freely of our time, our possessions, and, most especially, our love.

In 2 Corinthians 9, Paul reminds us that when we sow the seeds of generosity, we reap bountiful rewards in accordance with God's plan for our lives. But Paul offers a word of caution: We are commanded to be cheerful givers—not to give "grudgingly or under compulsion" (v. 7).

Today, take God's words to heart and make this pledge: be a cheerful, generous, courageous giver. The world needs your help, and you need the spiritual rewards that will be yours when you do.

What is your focus today? Joy comes when it is Jesus first, others second…then you.

Kay Arthur

Thoughts on Generosity

Selfishness is as far from Christianity
as darkness is from light.

C. H. Spurgeon

It is the duty of every Christian to be Christ
to his neighbor.

Martin Luther

Let us not lose heart in doing good, for in due time
we shall reap if we do not grow weary. So then,
while we have opportunity, let us do good to all
men, and especially to those who are of the
household of the faith.

Galatians 6:9-10 NASB

Lord, You have been so generous with me;
let me be generous with others. Help me to give
generously of my time and my possessions
as I care for those in need. And, make me
a humble giver, Lord, so that all the glory and
the praise might be Yours.

~Amen

Gifts

Do not neglect the spiritual gift
that is within you....

1 Timothy 4:14 NASB

All women possess special gifts and talents;
you are no exception. But, your gift is no guarantee
of success; it must be cultivated and nurtured;
otherwise, it will go unused...and God's gift to you
will be squandered.

Today, accept this challenge: value the talent
that God has given you, nourish it, make it grow,
and share it with the world. After all, the best way
to say "Thank You" for God's gift is to use it.

The Lord has abundantly blessed me all of my life.
I'm not trying to pay Him back for all of His
wonderful gifts; I just realize that He gave
them to me to give away.

Lisa Whelchel

Using Our Gifts

When God crowns our merits, he is crowning
nothing other than his gifts.

St. Augustine

Since we have gifts that differ according to
the grace given to us, let each exercise them
accordingly: if prophecy, according to the
proportion of his faith; if service, in his serving;
or he who teaches, in his teaching; or he who
exhorts, in his exhortation; he who gives, with
liberality; he who leads, with diligence;
he who shows mercy, with cheerfulness.

Romans 12:6-8 NASB

Lord, I praise You for Your priceless gifts. I give
thanks for Your creation, for Your Son, and for
the unique talents and opportunities that You have
given me. Let me use my gifts for the glory
of Your kingdom, this day and every day.

~Amen

God's Blessings

The LORD bless thee, and keep thee:
The LORD make his face shine upon thee,
and be gracious unto thee.

Numbers 6:24-25 KJV

If you sat down and began counting your blessings, how long would it take? A very, very long time! Your blessings include life, freedom, family, friends, talents, and possessions, for starters. But, your greatest blessing—a gift that is yours for the asking— is God's gift of salvation through Christ Jesus.

Today, begin making a list of your blessings. You most certainly will not be able to make a complete list, but take a few moments and jot down as many blessings as you can. Then give thanks to the Giver of all good things: God. His love for you is eternal, as are His gifts. And it's never too soon—or too late— to offer Him thanks.

We do not need to beg Him to bless us;
He simply cannot help it.

Hannah Whitall Smith

Count Your Blessings

Oh! what a Savior, gracious to all.
Oh! how His blessings round us fall.
Gently to comfort, kindly to cheer,
sleeping or waking, God is near.
Fanny Crosby

Think of the blessings we so easily take for
granted: Life itself; preservation from danger;
every bit of health we enjoy; every hour of liberty;
the ability to see, to hear, to speak, to think, and
to imagine all this comes from the hand of God.
Billy Graham

For thou, LORD, wilt bless the righteous....
Psalm 5:12 KJV

Lord, You have given me so much, and
I am thankful. Today, I seek Your blessings for my
life, and I know that every good thing You give me
is to be shared with others. I am blessed that I
might be a blessing to those around me, Father.
Let me give thanks for Your gifts . . .
and let me share them.
~Amen

God's Commandments

This is how we are sure that we have come to
know Him: by keeping His commands.

1 John 2:3 HCSB

A righteous life has many components: faith,
honesty, generosity, love, kindness, humility,
gratitude, and worship, to name but a few. If we seek
to follow the steps of our Savior, Jesus Christ, we
must seek to live according to His commandments.
In short, we must, to the best of our abilities, live
according to the principles contained in God's Holy
Word.

The Holy Bible contains thorough instructions
which, if followed, lead to fulfillment, righteousness,
and salvation. But, if we choose to ignore God's
commandments, the results are as predictable as they
are tragic. Let us follow God's commandments, and
let us conduct our lives in such a way that we might
be shining examples for those who have not yet found
Christ.

To yield to God means to belong to God, and
to belong to God means to have all His infinite
power. To belong to God means to have all.

Hannah Whitall Smith

Following God's Commands

Don't worry about what you do not understand.
Worry about what you do understand in
the Bible but do not live by.

Corrie ten Boom

Bible history is filled with people who began
the race with great success but failed at the end
because they disregarded God's rules.

Warren Wiersbe

Jesus answered and said unto him, If a man love
me, he will keep my words: and my Father will
love him, and we will come unto him,
and make our abode with him.

John 14:23 KJV

Lord, Your commandments are a perfect guide
for my life; let me obey them, and let me lead
others to do the same. Give me the wisdom to
walk righteously in Your way, Dear Lord,
trusting always in You.

~Amen

God's Faithfulness

For the LORD is good. His unfailing love
continues forever, and his faithfulness
continues to each generation.

Psalm 100:5 NLT

God is faithful to us even when we are not
faithful to Him. God keeps His promises to us even
when we stray far from His will. He continues to
love us even when we disobey His commandments.
But God does not force His blessings upon us. If we
are to experience His love and His grace, we must
claim them for ourselves.

Are you tired, discouraged, or fearful? Be
comforted: God is with you. Are you confused? Listen
to the quiet voice of your Heavenly Father. Are you
bitter? Talk with God and seek His guidance. Are
you celebrating a great victory? Thank God and
praise Him. He is the Giver of all things good.

In whatever condition you find yourself,
wherever you are, whether you are happy or sad,
victorious or vanquished, troubled or triumphant,
remember that God is faithful and that His love is
eternal. And be comforted. God is not just near. He
is here.

Thoughts on His Faithfulness

God's faithfulness has never depended on the faithfulness of his children…. God is greater than our weakness. In fact, I think, it is our weakness that reveals how great God is.

Max Lucado

There is no pit so deep that God's love is not deeper still.

Corrie ten Boom

Because of the LORD's great love we are not consumed, for his compassions never fail. They are new every morning; great is your faithfulness.

Lamentations 3:22-23 NIV

Lord, Your faithfulness is everlasting. You are faithful to me even when I am not faithful to You. Today, let me serve You faithfully, and let me rest in the knowledge of Your unchanging and constant love for me.

~Amen

Praise be to the God and Father of our Lord Jesus
Christ! In his great mercy he has given us new
birth into a living hope through the resurrection
of Jesus Christ from the dead.

1 Peter 1:3 NIV

God is merciful, and His love is boundless and
eternal. He sent His only Son to die for our sins. We
must praise God always and thank Him for His
priceless gifts.

Romans 3:23 reminds us of a universal truth: "All
have sinned, and come short of the glory of God"
(KJV). And, despite our imperfections, God sent His
Son to die so that we might have eternal life. As
Christians, we have been blessed by a merciful, loving
God, and one way that we thank our Creator is to
share His love and His mercy with our friends, with
our families, and with all whom God chooses to place
in our paths.

God is the light in my darkness,
the voice in my silence.

Helen Keller

Thoughts on His Mercy

Redeemed, how I love to proclaim it! Redeemed
by the blood of the Lamb; Redeemed through
His infinite mercy, His child, and forever, I am.

Fanny Crosby

God's mercy is infinite, but it always flows
to humanity through the golden channel
of Jesus Christ, his son.

C. H. Spurgeon

The LORD is good to all, and His mercies
are over all His works.

Psalm 145:9 NASB

Dear Lord, You have blessed me with so much:
Your love, Your mercy, and Your grace. Enable me
to be merciful toward others, Father, just as You
have been merciful toward me so that I might
share Your love with all who cross my path.

~Amen

God's Plan

And we know that in all things God works for the good of those who love him, who have been called according to his purpose.

Romans 8:28 NIV

God has plans for your life that are far grander than you can imagine. But He won't force you to follow His will; to the contrary, He has given you free will, the ability to make choices and decisions on your own. The most important decision of your life is, of course, your commitment to accept Jesus Christ as your personal Lord and Savior. And once your eternal destiny is secured, you will undoubtedly ask yourself "What now, Lord?" If you earnestly seek God's will for your life, you will find it…in time.

Sometimes, God's plans are crystal clear, but other times, He may lead you through the wilderness before He delivers you to the Promised Land. So be patient, keep praying, and keep seeking His will for your life. When you do, you'll be amazed at the marvelous things that an all-powerful, all-knowing God can do.

Every experience God gives us, every person He puts in our lives, is the perfect preparation for the future that only He can see.

Corrie ten Boom

Following God's Plan

The only thing that can hinder us is our own
failure to work in harmony with the plans of the
Creator, and if this lack of harmony can be
removed, then God can work.

Hannah Whitall Smith

We will stand amazed to see the topside of the
tapestry and how God beautifully embroidered
each circumstance into a pattern for
our good and His glory.

Joni Eareckson Tada

Now the God of peace . . . equip you
in every good thing to do His will.

Hebrews 13:20-21 NASB

Lord, today, I will seek Your will for my life.
You have a plan for me, Father. Let me discover it
and live it, knowing that when I trust in You,
I am eternally blessed.

~Amen

God's Promises

For you have need of endurance, so that
when you have done the will of God, you may
receive what was promised.

Hebrews 10:36 NASB

God's Word contains promises upon which
we, as Christians, can and must depend. The Bible
is a priceless gift, a tool that God intends for us to
use in every aspect of our lives. Too many Christians,
however, keep their spiritual tool kits tightly closed
and out of sight.

Are you tired? Discouraged? Fearful? Be
comforted and trust the promises that God has made
to you. Are you worried or anxious? Be confident in
God's power. He will never desert you. Do you see a
difficult future ahead? Be courageous and call upon
God. He will protect you and then use you according
to His purposes. Are you confused? Listen to the quiet
voice of your Heavenly Father. He is not a God of
confusion. Talk with Him; listen to Him; trust Him,
and trust His promises. He is steadfast, and He is
your Protector . . . forever.

Shake the dust from your past, and
move forward in His promises.

Kay Arthur

Thoughts on His Promises

We have ample evidence that the Lord is able
to guide. The promises cover every imaginable
situation. All we need to do is to take
the hand He stretches out.

Elisabeth Elliot

God's promises are overflowings from
His great heart.

C. H. Spurgeon

Let us hold on to the confession of our hope
without wavering, for He who promised is faithful.

Hebrews 10:23 HCSB

~

Lord, Your Holy Word contains promises, and
I will trust them. I will use the Bible as my guide,
and I will trust You, Lord, to speak to me through
Your Holy Spirit and through Your Holy Word,
this day and forever.

~Amen

God's Timing

He has made everything beautiful in its time.
He has also set eternity in the hearts of men;
yet they cannot fathom what God
has done from beginning to end.

Ecclesiastes 3:11 NIV

Sometimes, the hardest thing to do is to wait. This is especially true when we're in a hurry and when we want things to happen now, if not sooner! But God's plan does not always happen in the way that we would like or at the time of our own choosing. Our task—as believing Christians who trust in a benevolent, all-knowing Father—is to wait patiently for God to reveal Himself.

We human beings are, by nature, impatient. We know what we want, and we know exactly when we want it: RIGHT NOW! But, God knows better. He has created a world that unfolds according to His own timetable, not ours . . . thank goodness!

We must leave it to God to answer our prayers
in His own wisest way. Sometimes, we are so
impatient and think that God does not answer.
God always answers! He never fails!
Be still. Abide in Him.

Mrs. Charles E. Cowman

Thoughts on God's Timing

The stops of a good man are ordered by
the Lord as well as his steps.

George Mueller

He has the right to interrupt your life. He is Lord.
When you accepted Him as Lord, you gave
Him the right to help Himself to your life
anytime He wants.

Henry Blackaby

I trust in You, O LORD, I say, "You are my God."
My times are in Your hand.

Psalm 31:14-15 NASB

Dear Lord, Your wisdom is infinite, and the timing
of Your heavenly plan is perfect. You have a plan
for my life that is grander than I can imagine.
When I am impatient, remind me that
You are never early or late. You are always on time,
Father, so let me trust in You.

~Amen

God's Word

But He answered, "It is written: Man must not live on bread alone, but on every word that comes from the mouth of God."

Matthew 4:4 HCSB

God's Word is unlike any other book. The Bible is a roadmap for life here on earth and for life eternal. As Christians, we are called upon to study God's Holy Word, to trust its promises, to follow its commandments, and to share its good news with the world.

As believers, we must study the Bible daily and meditate upon its meaning for our lives. Otherwise, we deprive ourselves of a priceless gift from our Creator. God's Holy Word is, indeed, a transforming, life-changing, one-of-a-kind treasure. And, a passing acquaintance with the Good Book is insufficient for Christians who seek to obey God's Word and to understand His will. After all, neither man nor woman should live by bread alone....

God's Word is a light not only to our path but to our thinking. Place it in your heart today, and you will never walk in darkness.

Joni Eareckson Tada

Weave the unveiling fabric of God's word through
your heart and mind. It will hold strong,
even if the rest of life unravels.

Gigi Graham Tchividjian

Nobody ever outgrows Scripture; the book
widens and deepens with our years.

C. H. Spurgeon

Thy word is a lamp unto my feet, and
a light unto my path.

Psalm 119:105 KJV

Lord, You've given me instructions for life
here on earth and for life eternal. I will use the
Bible as my guide. I will study it and meditate
upon it as I trust You, Lord, to speak to me
through Your Holy Word.

~Amen

Grace

For it is by grace you have been saved, through faith—and this not from yourselves, it is the gift of God—not by works, so that no one can boast.

Ephesians 2:8-9 NIV

We have received countless gifts from God, but none can compare with the gift of salvation. When we accept Christ into our hearts, we are saved by God's grace. The familiar words of Ephesians 2:8 make God's promise perfectly clear: we are saved, not by our actions, but by God's mercy. We are saved, not because of our good deeds, but because of our faith in Christ.

God's grace is the ultimate gift, and we owe Him the ultimate in thanksgiving. Let us praise the Creator for His priceless gift, and let us share the good news with all who cross our paths. We return our Father's love by accepting His grace and by sharing His message and His love. When we do, we are blessed here on earth and throughout all eternity.

God does amazing works through prayers that seek to extend His grace to others.

Shirley Dobson

God's Gift of Grace

Though the details may differ from story to story,
we are all sinners—saved only by
the wonderful grace of God.

Gloria Gaither

Grace: a gift that costs everything for
the giver and nothing for the recipient.

Philip Yancey

For God so loved the world that he gave his one
and only Son, that whoever believes in him
shall not perish but have eternal life.

John 3:16 NIV

Lord, You have saved me by Your grace.
Keep me mindful that Your grace is a gift that I
can accept but cannot earn. I praise You for that
priceless gift, today and forever. Let me share the
good news of Your grace with a world that
desperately needs Your healing touch.

~Amen

Gratitude

As you therefore have received Christ Jesus the Lord, so walk in Him, having been firmly rooted and now being built up in Him and established in your faith, just as you were instructed, and overflowing with gratitude.

Colossians 2:6-7 NASB

For most of us, life is busy and complicated. We have countless responsibilities, some of which begin before sunrise and many of which end long after sunset. Amid the rush and crush of the daily grind, it is easy to lose sight of God and His blessings. But, when we forget to slow down and say "Thank You" to our Maker, we rob ourselves of His presence, His peace, and His joy.

Our task, as believing Christians, is to praise God many times each day. Then, with gratitude in our hearts, we can face our daily duties with the perspective and power that only He can provide.

Let's thank God for allowing us to experience troubles that drive us closer to Him.

Shirley Dobson

The Importance of a Grateful Heart

A spirit of thankfulness makes all the difference.
Billy Graham

It is only with gratitude that life becomes rich.
Dietrich Bonhoeffer

I have heard your prayer, I have seen your tears;
behold, I will heal you.
2 Kings 20:5 NASB

Lord, let my attitude be one of gratitude. You have
given me much; when I think of Your grace and
goodness, I am humbled and thankful. Today, let
me express my thanksgiving, Father, not just
through my words but also through my deeds . . .
and may all the glory be Yours.
~Amen

Delight thyself also in the LORD; and he shall give
thee the desires of thine heart.

Psalm 37:4 KJV

Happiness depends less upon our circumstances
than upon our thoughts. When we turn our thoughts
to God, to His gifts, and to His glorious creation, we
experience the joy that God intends for His children.
But, when we focus on the negative aspects of life,
we suffer needlessly.

Do you sincerely want to be a happy Christian?
Then set your mind and your heart upon God's love
and His grace. The fullness of life in Christ is
available to all who seek it and claim it. Count
yourself among that number. Seek first the salvation
available through a personal relationship with Jesus
Christ, and then claim the joy, the peace, and the
spiritual abundance that the Shepherd offers His
sheep.

Those who are God's without reserve are,
in every sense, content.

Hannah Whitall Smith

On Being a Happy Christian

Make God's will the focus of your life day by day.
If you seek to please Him and Him alone,
you'll find yourself satisfied with life.

Kay Arthur

The secret of a happy life is to delight in duty.
When duty becomes delight,
then burdens become blessings.

Warren Wiersbe

Thou wilt show me the path of life:
in thy presence is fulness of joy; at thy right hand
there are pleasures for evermore.

Psalm 16:11 KJV

Dear Lord, I will rejoice in the day that You have
made, and I will give thanks for the countless
blessings that You have given me. Let me be a
joyful Christian, Father, as I share the good news
of Your Son, and let me praise You for all
the marvelous things you have done.

~Amen

Honesty

You shall not steal, nor deal falsely,
nor lie to one another.

Leviticus 19:11 NASB

As the familiar saying goes, "Honesty is the best policy." For believers, it is far more important to note that honesty is God's policy. And if we are to be servants worthy of our savior, Jesus Christ, we must be honest and forthright in our communications with others.

Sometimes, honesty is difficult; sometimes, honesty is painful; but always honesty is God's commandment. In the Book of Exodus, God did not command, "Thou shalt not bear false witness when it is convenient." God said, "Thou shalt not bear false witness against thy neighbor." Period.

Sometime soon, perhaps even today, you will be tempted to bend the truth or perhaps even break it. Resist that temptation. Truth is God's way, and it must also be yours. Period.

The single most important element in any human relationship is honesty—with oneself, with God, and with others.

Catherine Marshall

Thoughts on Honesty

Honesty has a beautiful and refreshing simplicity about it. No ulterior motives. No hidden meanings. As honesty and integrity characterize our lives, there will be no need to manipulate others.

Charles Swindoll

You cannot glorify Christ and practice deception at the same time.

Warren Wiersbe

And put on the new self, which in the likeness of God has been created in righteousness and holiness of the truth. Therefore, laying aside falsehood, speak truth, each one of you, with his neighbor, for we are members of one another.

Ephesians 4:24-25 NASB

Dear Lord, You command Your children to walk in truth. Let me follow Your commandment. Give me the courage to speak honestly, and let me walk righteously with You so that others might see Your eternal truth reflected in my words and my deeds.

~Amen

Hope

For I hope in You, O LORD;
You will answer, O Lord my God.

Psalm 38:15 NASB

Despite God's promises, despite Christ's love, and despite our countless blessings, we frail human beings can still lose hope from time to time. When we do, we need the encouragement of Christian friends, the life-changing power of prayer, and the healing truth of God's Holy Word. If we find ourselves falling into the spiritual traps of worry and discouragement, we should seek the healing touch of Jesus and the encouraging words of fellow Christians.

Even though this world can be a place of trials and struggles, God has promised us peace, joy, and eternal life if we give ourselves to Him. And, of course, God keeps His promises today, tomorrow, and forever.

Love is the seed of all hope. It is the enticement to trust, to risk, to try, and to go on.

Gloria Gaither

Thoughts on Hope

No other religion, no other philosophy promises
new bodies, hearts, and minds. Only in
the Gospel of Christ do hurting people
find such incredible hope.

Joni Eareckson Tada

Hope is no other than the expectation
of those things which faith has believed
to be truly promised by God.

John Calvin

This hope we have as an anchor of the soul,
a hope both sure and steadfast.

Hebrews 6:19 NASB

Lord, I will place my hope in You. If I become
discouraged, I will turn to You. If I am afraid,
I will seek strength in You. In every aspect of my
life, I will trust You. You are my Father, and I will
place my hope and my faith in You.

~Amen

Joy

May the God of hope fill you with all joy and peace as you trust in him, so that you may overflow with hope by the power of the Holy Spirit.

Romans 15:13 NIV

As believers, we have every reason to celebrate. Yet sometimes, amid the inevitable hustle and bustle of life here on earth, we can forfeit—albeit temporarily—the joy that God intends for our lives.

The familiar words of the 100th Psalm encourage us to "Shout for joy to the LORD, all the earth. Worship the LORD with gladness" (vv. 1-2 NIV). C. H. Spurgeon reminds us that "Rejoicing is clearly a spiritual command. To ignore it is disobedience." As Christians, we are called by our Creator to live abundantly, prayerfully, and joyfully. To do otherwise is to squander His spiritual gifts.

If, today, your heart is heavy, open the door of your soul to the Father and to His only begotten Son. Christ offers you His peace and His joy. Accept it and share it freely, just as Christ has freely shared His joy with you.

God knows everything. He can manage everything, and He loves us. Surely this is enough for a fullness of joy that is beyond words.

Hannah Whitall Smith

Our hope in Christ for the future is
the mainstream of our joy.
C. H. *Spurgeon*

There is not one blade of grass, there is no color in
this world that is not intended to make us rejoice.
John Calvin

Rejoice, and be exceeding glad:
for great is your reward in heaven....
Matthew 5:12 KJV

Dear Lord, You have created a glorious universe
that is far beyond my understanding. You have
given me the gift of Your Son and the gift of
salvation. Let me be a joyful Christian, Lord, this
day and every day. Today is Your gift to me. Let me
use it to Your glory as I give all the praise to You.
~*Amen*

Kindness

So, as those who have been chosen of God, holy
and beloved, put on a heart of compassion,
kindness, humility, gentleness and patience.

Colossians 3:12 NASB

For Christian believers, kindness is not an option; it is a commandment. In the Gospel of Matthew, Jesus declares, "In everything, therefore, treat people the same way you want them to treat you, for this is the Law and the Prophets" (Matthew 7:12 NASB). Jesus did not say, "In some things, treat people as you wish to be treated." And, He did not say, "From time to time, treat others with kindness." Christ said that we should treat others as we wish to be treated in everything. This, of course, is a tall order indeed, but as Christians, we are commanded to do our best.

Today, as you consider all the things that Christ has done in your life, honor Him by following His commandment and obeying the Golden Rule. He expects no less, and He deserves no less.

All kindness and good deeds, we must keep silent.
The result will be an inner reservoir
of personality power.

Catherine Marshall

Thoughts on the Golden Rule

Do all the good you can. By all the means you can.
In all the ways you can. In all the places you can.
At all the times you can. To all the people you
can. As long as ever you can.

John Wesley

When you extend hospitality to others,
you're not trying to impress people;
you're trying to reflect God to them.

Max Lucado

And as ye would that men should do to you,
do ye also to them likewise.

Luke 6:31 KJV

Help me, Lord, to see the needs of those
around me. Today, let me spread kind words of
thanksgiving and celebration in honor of Your
Son. Today, let forgiveness rule my heart. And
every day, Lord, let my love for Christ be reflected
through deeds of kindness for those who need
the healing touch of the Master's hand.

~Amen

Laughter

A joyful heart is good medicine.

Proverbs 17:22 NASB

Laughter is medicine for the soul, but sometimes, amid the stresses of the day, we forget to take our medicine. Instead of viewing our world with a mixture of optimism and humor, we allow worries and distractions to rob us of the joy that God intends for our lives.

Today, as you go about your daily activities, approach life with a smile and a chuckle. After all, God created laughter for a reason…and Father indeed knows best. So laugh!

Laughter dulls the sharpest pain and flattens
out the greatest stress. To share it is
to give a gift of health.

Barbara Johnson

Humor ought to be consecrated and
used for the cause of Christ.

C. H. Spurgeon

A keen sense of humor helps us to overlook
the unbecoming, understand the unconventional,
tolerate the unpleasant, overcome
the unexpected, and outlast the unbearable.

Billy Graham

Shout joyfully to the LORD, all the earth;
break forth in song, rejoice, and sing praises.

Psalm 98:4-6 NASB

Lord, when I begin to take myself or my life too
seriously, let me laugh. When I rush from place to
place, slow me down, Lord, and let me laugh.
Put a smile on my face, Dear Lord, and let me
share that smile with all who cross my path . . .
and let me laugh.

~Amen

Love

But now abide faith, hope, love, these three;
but the greatest of these is love.

1 Corinthians 13:13 NASB

The familiar words of 1 Corinthians 13 remind us that love is God's commandment. Faith is important, of course. So too is hope. But love is more important still.

Christ demonstrated His love for us on the cross, and, as Christians, we are called upon to return Christ's love by sharing it. Sometimes love is easy (puppies and sleeping children come to mind) and sometimes love is hard (fallible human beings come to mind). But God's Word is clear: we are to love all of our neighbors, not just the lovable ones. So today, take time to spread Christ's message by word and by example. And the greatest of these is example.

Love is the seed of all hope.
It is the enticement to trust, to risk, to try,
and to go on.

Gloria Gaither

A Loving Heart

It is when we come to the Lord in
our nothingness, our powerlessness and our
helplessness that He then enables us to love
in a way which, without Him, would be
absolutely impossible.

Elisabeth Elliot

Love is an attribute of God. To love others is
evidence of a genuine faith.

Kay Arthur

If we love one another, God abides in us,
and His love is perfected in us.

1 John 4:12 NASB

Lord, You have given me the gift of eternal love;
let me share that gift. Help me, Father, to show
tenderness and unfailing love to my family
and friends. Make me generous with words
of encouragement and praise. And, help me always
to reflect the love that Christ Jesus gave me
so that through me, others might find Him.

~Amen

Loving God

You shall love the LORD your God with
all your heart and with all your soul and
with all your might.

Deuteronomy 6:5 NASB

When we worship God with faith and
assurance, we place Him at the absolute center of
our lives. We invite His love into our hearts. In turn,
we grow to love Him more deeply as we sense His
love for us. St. Augustine wrote, "I love you, Lord,
not doubtingly, but with absolute certainty. Your
Word beat upon my heart until I fell in love with
you, and now the universe and everything in it tells
me to love you."

Today, let us pray that we, too, will turn our
hearts to our Father, knowing with certainty that
He loves us and that we love Him.

Telling the Lord how much you love Him
and why is what praise and worship are all about.

Lisa Whelchel

When We Love Our Creator

I love you, Lord, not doubtingly, but with absolute
certainty. Your Word beat upon my heart until
I fell in love with you, and now the universe and
everything in it tells me to love you, and tells
the same thing to us all.

St. Augustine

In true religion, to love God and to know
God are synonymous terms.

C. H. Spurgeon

And we know that all things work together
for good to them that love God, to them who are
the called according to his purpose.

Romans 8:28 KJV

Dear Lord, You have blessed me with a love that is
infinite and eternal. Let me love You, Lord, more
and more each day. Make me a loving servant,
Father, today and throughout eternity. And, let me
show my love for You by sharing Your message
and Your love with others.

~Amen

Patience

So, as those who have been chosen of God,
holy and beloved, put on a heart of compassion,
kindness, humility, gentleness and patience.

Colossians 3:12 NASB

Life demands patience . . . and lots of it! We live in an imperfect world inhabited by imperfect people. Sometimes, we inherit troubles from others, and sometimes we create trouble for ourselves. In either case, what's required is patience.

Lamentations 3:25-26 reminds us that, "The LORD is wonderfully good to those who wait for him and seek him. So it is good to wait quietly for salvation from the LORD" (NLT). But, for most of us, waiting quietly for God is difficult. Why? Because we are fallible human beings, sometimes quick to anger and sometimes slow to forgive.

The next time you find your patience tested to the limit, remember that the world unfolds according to God's timetable, not ours. Sometimes, we must wait patiently, and that's as it should be. After all, think how patient God has been with us.

A Patient Heart

Wait on the Lord, wait patiently, And thou shalt
in Him be blest; After the storm, a holy calm,
And after thy labor rest.

Fanny Crosby

We must learn to wait.
There is grace supplied to the one who waits.

Mrs. Charles E. Cowman

We urge you, brethren, admonish the unruly,
encourage the fainthearted, help the weak,
be patient with everyone.

1 Thessalonians 5:14 NASB

Dear Lord, give me patience. Let me live
according to Your plan and according to Your
timetable. When I am hurried, slow me down.
When I become impatient with others, give me
empathy. When I am frustrated by the demands
of the day, give me peace. Today, let me be
a patient Christian, Lord, as I trust in You and
in Your master plan for my life.

~Amen

Peace

Peace I leave with you; My peace I give to you;
not as the world gives do I give to you.
Do not let your heart be troubled,
nor let it be fearful.

John 14:27 NASB

The beautiful words of John 14:27 promise us
that Jesus offers us peace, not as the world gives, but
as He alone gives. We, as believers, can accept His
peace or ignore it. When we accept the peace of Jesus
Christ into our hearts, our lives are transformed. And
then, because we possess the gift of peace, we can
share that gift with fellow Christians, family
members, friends, and associates. If, on the other
hand, we choose to ignore the gift of peace—for
whatever reason—we simply cannot share what we
do not possess.

Today, as a gift to yourself, to your family, and to
your friends, claim the inner peace that is your
spiritual birthright: the peace of Jesus Christ. It is
offered freely; it has been paid for in full; it is yours
for the asking. So ask. And then share.

God's Peace

Rejoicing is a matter of obedience to God—
an obedience that will start you on the road to
peace and contentment.

Kay Arthur

There may be no trumpet sound or loud applause
when we make a right decision, just a calm sense
of resolution and peace.

Gloria Gaither

And let the peace of God rule in your hearts…
and be ye thankful.

Colossians 3:15 KJV

Dear Lord, the peace that the world offers is
fleeting, but You offer a peace that is perfect and
eternal. Let me turn the cares and burdens of
my life over to You, Father, and let me feel
the spiritual abundance that You offer through
the person of Your Son, the Prince of Peace.

~Amen

93

Possessions

Lay not up for yourselves treasures upon earth,
where moth and rust doth corrupt, and where
thieves break through and steal: but lay up for
yourselves treasures in heaven, where neither
moth nor rust doth corrupt, and where thieves
do not break through nor steal: for where your
treasure is, there will your heart be also.

Matthew 6:19-21 KJV

On the grand stage of a well-lived life, material
possessions should play a rather small role. Of course,
we all need the basic necessities of life, but once we
meet those needs for ourselves and for our families,
the piling up of possessions creates more problems
than it solves. Our real riches, of course, are not of
this world. We are never really rich until we are rich
in spirit.

Do you find yourself wrapped up in the concerns
of the material world? If so, it's time to reorder your
priorities by turning your thoughts and your prayers
to more important matters. And, it's time to begin
storing up riches that will endure throughout eternity:
the spiritual kind.

No one is truly happy if he has what he wants, but
only if he wants something he should have.

St. Augustine

Earthly Treasures and Spiritual Riches

I have held many things in my hands, and
I have lost them all; but whatever I have placed in
God's hands, that I still possess.

Corrie ten Boom

Hold everything earthly with a loose hand, but
grasp eternal things with a deathlike grip.

C. H. Spurgeon

No man can serve two masters: for either he will
hate the one, and love the other; or else he will
hold to the one, and despise the other.
Ye cannot serve God and mammon.

Matthew 6:24 KJV

Lord, my greatest possession is my relationship
with You through Jesus Christ. You have promised
that when I first seek Your kingdom and Your
righteousness You will give me whatever I need.
Let me trust You completely, Lord, for my needs,
both material and spiritual, this day and always.

~Amen

Prayer

Be anxious for nothing, but in everything by
prayer and supplication with thanksgiving
let your requests be made known to God.

Philippians 4:6 NASB

"The power of prayer": these words are so
familiar, yet sometimes we forget what they mean.
Prayer is a powerful tool for communicating with
our Creator; it is an opportunity to commune with
the Giver of all things good. Prayer is not a thing to
be taken lightly or to be used infrequently.

All too often, amid the rush of daily life, we may
lose sight of God's presence in our lives. Instead of
turning to Him for guidance and for comfort, we
depend, instead, upon our own resources. To do so is
a profound mistake.

Today, instead of turning things over in your
mind, turn them over to God in prayer. Instead of
worrying about your decisions, trust God to help you
make them. Pray constantly about things great and
small. God is listening, and He wants to hear from
you. Now.

When there is a matter that requires definite
prayer, pray until you believe God and until you
can thank Him for His answer.

Hannah Whitall Smith

Don't be overwhelmed…take it one day
and one prayer at a time.

Stormie Omartian

Prayer is our pathway not only to divine
protection, but also to a personal,
intimate relationship with God.

Shirley Dobson

The intense prayer of the righteous is
very powerful.

James 5:16 HCSB

I pray to You, my Heavenly Father, because
You desire it and because I need it. Prayer not only
changes things; it changes me. Help me, Lord,
never to face the demands of the day without
first spending time with You.

~Amen

Relationships

Beloved, if God so loved us,
we also ought to love one another.

1 John 4:11 NASB

As we travel along life's road, we build lifelong relationships with a small, dear circle of family and friends. And how best do we build and maintain these relationships? By following the Word of God.

Healthy relationships are built upon honesty, compassion, responsible behavior, trust, and optimism. Healthy relationships are built upon the Golden Rule. Healthy relationships are built upon sharing and caring. All of these principles are found time and time again in God's Holy Word. When we read God's Word, when we follow His commandments, and when we trust His promises, we enrich our own lives and the lives of those we love.

Line by line, moment by moment, special times
are etched into our memories in the permanent
ink of everlasting love in our relationships.

Gloria Gaither

Our attitude determines our relationships
with people.
John Maxwell

It is the duty of every Christian to be Christ
to his neighbor.
Martin Luther

May the Lord cause you to increase and abound
in love for one another, and for all people.
1 Thessalonians 3:12 NASB

Dear Lord, You have brought family members
and friends into my life. Let me love them,
let me help them, let me treasure them, and
let me lead them to You.
~Amen

Renewal

Those who hope in the LORD will renew
their strength. They will soar on wings like eagles;
they will run and not grow weary,
they will walk and not be faint.

Isaiah 40:31 NIV

For busy women living in a fast-paced 21st century world, life may seem like a merry-go-round that never stops turning. If that description seems to fit your life, then you may find yourself running short of patience or strength or both. If you're feeling tired or discouraged, there is a source from which you can draw the power needed to recharge your spiritual batteries. That source is God.

Are you exhausted or troubled? Turn your heart toward God in prayer. Are you weak or worried? Take the time—or, more accurately, make the time—to delve deeply into God's Holy Word. Are you spiritually depleted? Call upon fellow believers to support you, and call upon Christ to renew your spirit and your life. When you do, you'll discover that the Creator of the universe stands always ready and always able to create a new sense of wonderment and joy in you.

He is the God of wholeness and restoration.

Stormie Omartian

Relying on God

Jesus is calling the weary to rest, Calling today,
calling today, Bring Him your burden and
you shall be blest; He will not turn you away.

Fanny Crosby

Repentance removes old sins and wrong attitudes,
and it opens the way for the Holy Spirit
to restore our spiritual health.

Shirley Dobson

Create in me a clean heart, O God;
and renew a right spirit within me.

Psalm 51:10 KJV

Dear Lord, sometimes I am troubled, and
sometimes I grow weary. When I am weak, Lord,
give me strength. When I am discouraged, renew
me. When I am fearful, let me feel Your healing
touch. Let me always trust in Your promises, Lord,
and let me draw strength from those promises and
from Your unending love.

~Amen

God is our refuge and strength,
a very present help in trouble.

Psalm 46:1 KJV

Some days are light and happy, and some days are not. When we face the inevitable dark days of life, we must choose how we will respond. Will we allow ourselves to sink even more deeply into our own sadness, or will we do the difficult work of pulling ourselves out?

We bring light to the dark days of life by turning first to God, and then to trusted family members and friends. Then, we must go to work solving the problems that confront us. When we do, the clouds will eventually part, and the sun will shine once more upon our souls.

We are never stronger than the moment
we admit we are weak.

Beth Moore

Finding Strength in God

Even in the winter, even in the midst of the storm,
the sun is still there. Somewhere, up above the
clouds, it still shines and warms and pulls at the
life buried deep inside the brown branches and
frozen earth. The sun is there! Spring will come.

Gloria Gaither

When all else is gone, God is still left.
Nothing changes Him.

Hannah Whitall Smith

Let not your heart be troubled;
ye believe in God, believe also in me.

John 14:1 KJV

Dear Heavenly Father, on those days when I am
troubled, You comfort me if I turn my thoughts
and prayers to You. When I am afraid, You protect
me. When I am discouraged, You lift me up.
You are my unending source of strength, Lord.
In every circumstance, let me trust Your plan
and Your will for my life.

~Amen

Serving Others

Your attitude should be the same as that
of Christ Jesus...taking the very nature
of a servant.

Philippians 2:5,7 NIV

We live in a world that glorifies power,
prestige, fame, and money. But the words of Jesus
teach us that the most esteemed men and women in
this world are not the self-congratulatory leaders of
society but are instead the humblest of servants.

Today, you may feel the temptation to build
yourself up in the eyes of your neighbors. Resist that
temptation. Instead, serve your neighbors quietly and
without fanfare. Find a need and fill it . . . humbly.
Lend a helping hand...anonymously. Share a word
of kindness . . . with quiet sincerity. As you go about
your daily activities, remember that the Savior of all
humanity made Himself a servant, and we, as His
followers, must do no less.

Love is an attribute of God. To love others is
evidence of a genuine faith.

Kay Arthur

On Serving Others

God wants us to serve Him with a willing spirit,
one that would choose no other way.

Beth Moore

Employ whatever God has entrusted you with,
in doing good, all possible good,
in every possible kind and degree.

John Wesley

But whosoever will be great among you, let him be
your minister; and whosoever will be chief among
you, let him be your servant: even as the Son of
man came not to be ministered unto, but to
minister, and to give his life a ransom for many.

Matthew 20:26-28 KJV

Father in heaven, when Jesus humbled Himself
and became a servant, He also became an example
for His followers. Today, as I serve my family
and friends, I do so in the name of Jesus, my Lord
and Master. Guide my steps, Father,
and let my service be pleasing to You.

~Amen

Spiritual Gifts

But the fruit of the Spirit is love, joy, peace, long-suffering, gentleness, goodness, faith, meekness, temperance: against such there is no law.

Galatians 5:22-23 KJV

All of us have spiritual gifts, and if we're wise, we continue to refine those gifts every day. The journey toward spiritual maturity lasts a lifetime. As Christians, we can and should continue to grow in the love and the knowledge of our Savior as long as we live. When we cease to grow, either emotionally or spiritually, we do ourselves a profound disservice. But, if we study God's Word, if we obey His commandments, and if we live in the center of His will, we will not be "stagnant" believers; we will, instead, be growing Christians . . . and that's exactly what God intends for us to be.

Life is a series of choices and decisions. Each day, we make countless decisions that can bring us closer to God . . . or not. When we live according to the principles contained in God's Holy Word, we embark upon a journey of spiritual maturity that results in life abundant and life eternal.

Using Your Spiritual Gifts

The maturity of a Christian experience cannot be
reached in a moment, but is the result of the work
of God's Holy Spirit, who, by His energizing
and transforming power, causes us to grow up
into Christ in all things.

Hannah Whitall Smith

Now there are varieties of gifts, but the same
Spirit. And there are varieties of ministries,
and the same Lord.

1 Corinthians 12:4-5 NASB

Dear Lord, Your richest gifts are spiritual, not
material. The Holy Scripture tells me that You are
at work in my life, continuing to help me grow
and to mature in the faith. Show me Your wisdom,
Father, and let me live according to
Your Word and Your will.

~Amen

Stress

Be of good courage, and he shall strengthen
your heart, all ye that hope in the LORD.

Psalm 31:24 KJV

Stressful days are an inevitable fact of modern
life. And how do we best cope with the challenges
of our demanding, 21st-century world? By turning
our days and our lives over to God. Elisabeth Elliot
writes, "If my life is surrendered to God, all is well.
Let me not grab it back, as though it were in peril in
His hand but would be safer in mine!" Yet even the
most devout Christian woman may, at times, seek to
grab the reins of her life and proclaim, "I'm in
charge!" To do so is foolish, prideful, and stressful.

When we seek to impose our own wills upon
the world—or upon other people—we invite stress
into our lives . . . needlessly. But, when we turn our
lives and our hearts over to God—when we accept
His will instead of seeking vainly to impose our
own—we discover the inner peace that can be ours
through Him.

Do you feel overwhelmed by the stresses of daily
life? Turn your concerns and your prayers over to
God. Trust Him. He knows your needs and will meet
those needs in His own way and in His own time if
you let Him.

God knows what each of us is dealing with.
He knows our pressures. He knows our conflicts.
And, He has made a provision for each and every
one of them. That provision is Himself in the
person of the Holy Spirit, dwelling in us
and empowering us to respond rightly.

Kay Arthur

Cast your burden upon the LORD and
He will sustain you: He will never allow
the righteous to be shaken.

Psalm 55:22 NASB

Heavenly Father, You never leave or forsake me.
Even when I am troubled by the demands of
the day, You are always with me, protecting me
and encouraging me. Whatever today may bring,
I thank You for Your love and Your strength.
Let me lean upon You, Father, this day and forever.

~Amen

Temptation

Your adversary, the devil, prowls around like
a roaring lion, seeking someone to devour.

1 Peter 5:8 NASB

How hard is it to bump into temptation in this crazy world? Not very hard. The devil, it seems, is working overtime these days while causing pain and heartache in more places and in more ways than ever before. We, as Christians, must remain vigilant. Not only must we resist Satan when he confronts us, but we must also avoid those places where Satan can most easily tempt us.

As believing Christians, we must beware, and we must earnestly wrap ourselves in the protection of God's Holy Word. When we do, we are secure.

Because Christ has faced our every temptation
without sin, we never face a temptation
that has no door of escape.

Beth Moore

Thoughts on Temptation

Since you are tempted without ceasing,
pray without ceasing.
C. H. Spurgeon

It is not the Word hidden in the head that keeps
us from sin. It is the Word hidden in the heart.
Vance Havner

The Lord knoweth how to deliver
the godly out of temptations....
2 Peter 2:9 KJV

Dear Lord, this world is filled with temptations,
distractions, and frustrations. When I turn my
thoughts away from You and Your Word, Lord,
I suffer bitter consequences. But, when I trust in
Your commandments, I am safe. Direct my path far
from the temptations and distractions of the world.
Let me discover Your will and follow it,
Dear Lord, this day and always.
~Amen

Thanksgiving

Make a joyful noise unto the LORD all ye lands.
Serve the LORD with gladness: come before his
presence with singing. Know ye that the LORD he
is God: it is he that hath made us, and not we
ourselves; we are his people and the sheep
of his pasture. Enter into his gates with
thanksgiving, and into his courts with praise;
be thankful unto him and bless his name
For the LORD is good; his mercy is everlasting;
and his truth endureth to all generations.

Psalm 100 KJV

As believing Christians, we are blessed
beyond measure. God sent His only Son to die for
our sins. And, God has given us the priceless gifts of
eternal love and eternal life. We, in turn, are
instructed to approach our Heavenly Father with
reverence and thanksgiving. But, we may sometimes
fail to pause and thank our Creator for the countless
blessings He has bestowed upon us. When we slow
down and express our gratitude to the One who made
us, we enrich our own lives and the lives of those
around us. Thanksgiving should become a habit, a
regular part of our daily routines. Yes, God has blessed
us beyond measure, and we owe Him everything,
including our eternal praise.

A Thankful Heart

God has promised that if we harvest well with
the tools of thanksgiving, there will be seeds
for planting in the spring.

Gloria Gaither

Why wait until the fourth Thursday in November?
Why wait until the morning of December
twenty-fifth? Thanksgiving to God should be
an everyday affair. The time to be thankful is now!

Jim Gallery

I will praise the name of God with a song,
and will magnify him with thanksgiving.

Psalm 69:30 KJV

Dear Lord, Your gifts are greater than I can
imagine. May I live each day with thanksgiving in
my heart and praise on my lips. Thank You for
the gift of Your Son and for the promise of eternal
life. Let me share the joyous news of Jesus Christ,
and let my life be a testimony to His love
and His grace.

~Amen

This is the day which the LORD has made;
let us rejoice and be glad in it.

Psalm 118:24 NASB

The familiar words of Psalm 118:24 remind us that every day is a gift from God. Yet on some days, we don't feel much like celebrating. When the obligations of everyday living seem to overwhelm us, we may find ourselves frustrated by the demands of the present and worried by the uncertainty of the future.

Each day is a special treasure to be savored and celebrated. May we—as believers who have so much to celebrate—never fail to praise our Creator by rejoicing in His glorious creation.

Submit each day to God, knowing that
He is God over all your tomorrows.

Kay Arthur

Every Day Is a Gift from God

Commitment to His lordship on Easter, at revivals,
or even every Sunday is not enough. We must
choose this day—and every day—whom we
will serve. This deliberate act of the will is
the inevitable choice between habitual
fellowship and habitual failure.

Beth Moore

It is good to give thanks to the LORD , to sing
praises to the Most High. It is good to proclaim
your unfailing love in the morning,
your faithfulness in the evening.

Psalm 92:1-2 NLT

Lord, You have given me another day of life;
let me celebrate this day, and let me use it
according to Your plan. I praise You, Father, for
my life and for the friends and family members
who make it rich. Enable me to live each moment
to the fullest as I give thanks for Your creation,
for Your love, and for Your Son.

~Amen

Trusting God

Trust in the LORD with all thine heart; and lean not unto thine own understanding. In all thy ways acknowledge him, and he shall direct thy paths.

Proverbs 3:5-6 KJV

The journey through life takes us over many peaks and through many valleys. When we reach the mountaintops, we find it easy to praise God and to give thanks. As we reach the crest of the mountain's peak, we trust God's plan. But, when we find ourselves in the dark valleys of life, when we face disappointment and despair, it is so much more difficult to trust God. But, trust Him we must.

As Christians, we can be comforted: whether we find ourselves at the pinnacle of the mountain or the darkest depths of the valley, God is there.

The next time you find your courage tested to the limit, lean upon God's promises. Trust His Son. Remember that God is always near and that He is your protector and your deliverer. When you are worried, anxious, or afraid, call upon Him. Remember that God rules both mountaintops and valleys—with limitless wisdom and love—now and forever.

Trusting the Father

Never be afraid to trust an unknown future
to a known God.

Corrie ten Boom

Let me encourage you to continue to wait with
faith. God may not perform a miracle, but He is
trustworthy to touch you and make you whole
where there used to be a hole.

Lisa Whelchel

The LORD is my rock, and my fortress,
and my deliverer; my God, my strength,
in whom I will trust....

Psalm 18:2 KJV

Today, Lord, I will trust You and seek Your will
for my life. You have a plan for me, Father.
Let me discover it and live it, knowing that
when I trust in You, I am eternally blessed.

~Amen

Truth

And ye shall know the truth,
and the truth shall make you free.

John 8:32 KJV

The words of John 8:32 are both familiar and profound: the truth, indeed, will make you free. Truth is God's way: He commands His children to live in truth, and He rewards those who follow His commandment. Jesus is the personification of a perfect, liberating truth that offers salvation to mankind.

Do you seek to walk with God? Do you seek to feel God's peace? Then you must walk in truth, and you must walk with the Savior. There is simply no other way.

Those who walk in truth walk in liberty.

Beth Moore

God's Truth

If you want the truth to go round the world you must hire an express train to pull it, but if you want a lie to go round the world, it will fly; it is as light as a feather, and a breath will carry it. It is well said in the old proverb, "A lie will go round the world while truth is putting its boots on."

C. H. Spurgeon

Peace, if possible, but truth at any rate.

Martin Luther

Teach me Your way, O LORD;
I will walk in Your truth.

Psalm 86:11 NASB

Dear Lord, let me trust in Your Word and in Your Son. Jesus said He was the truth, and I believe Him. Make Jesus the standard for truth in my life so that I might be a worthy example to others and a worthy servant to You.

~Amen

Wisdom

How much better to get wisdom than gold,
to choose understanding rather than silver!

Proverbs 16:16 NIV

Wisdom is not like a mushroom; it does not spring up overnight. It is, instead, like an oak tree that starts as a tiny acorn, grows into a sapling, and eventually reaches up to the sky, tall and strong. To become wise, we must seek God's wisdom and live according to His Word. And, we must not only learn the lessons of the Christian life, but we must also live by them.

Do you seek to live a life of righteousness and wisdom? If so, you must study the ultimate source of wisdom: the Word of God. You must seek out worthy mentors and listen carefully to their advice. You must associate, day in and day out, with godly men and women. And, you must act in accordance with your beliefs. When you study God's Word and live according to His commandments, you will become wise . . . and you will be a blessing to your friends, to your family, and to the world.

The doorstep to the temple of wisdom
is a knowledge of our own ignorance.

C. H. Spurgeon

Thoughts on God's Wisdom

Here is our opportunity: we cannot see God,
but we can see Christ. Christ was not only
the Son of God, but He was the Father.
Whatever Christ was, that God is.

Hannah Whitall Smith

Love Holy Scripture, and wisdom will love you.
Love Scripture, and she will keep you.
Honor her, and she will keep you.

St. Augustine

For the LORD giveth wisdom: out of his mouth
cometh knowledge and understanding.

Proverbs 2:6 KJV

Lord, make me a woman of wisdom and
discernment. I seek wisdom, Lord, not as the world
gives, but as You give. Lead me in Your ways and
teach me from Your Word so that, in time, my
wisdom might glorify Your kingdom and Your Son.

~Amen

Worry

Let not your heart be troubled:
ye believe in God, believe also in me.

John 14:1 KJV

Because we are fallible human beings, we worry. Even though we, as Christians, have the assurance of salvation—even though we, as Christians, have the promise of God's love and protection—we find ourselves fretting over the countless details of everyday life.

Perhaps you are concerned about the inevitable demands of the day ahead. Perhaps you are uncertain about your future or your finances. Or perhaps you are simply a "worrier" by nature. If so, it's time to turn your concerns over to a far higher power: God. He is still in His heaven, and you are His beloved child. God wants you to worry less and to trust Him more. Take your troubles to Him, and your fears, and your sorrows. Seek protection from the One who cannot be moved.

Remember always that there are two things which are more utterly incompatible even than oil and water, and these two are trust and worry.

Hannah Whitall Smith

Anxiety may be natural and normal for the world,
but it is not to be part of a believer's lifestyle.

Kay Arthur

Any concern that is too small to be turned into
a prayer is too small to be made into a burden.

Corrie ten Boom

Is anyone among you suffering?
Then he must pray.

James 5:13 NASB

Lord, You understand my worries and my fears,
and You forgive me when I am weak. When my
faith begins to wane, help me to trust You more.
Then, let me live courageously, faithfully,
prayerfully, and thankfully today and every day.

~Amen

Worship

I was glad when they said unto me,
Let us go into the house of the LORD.

Psalm 122:1 KJV

All of mankind is engaged in worship...of one kind or another. The question is not whether we worship, but what we worship. Some of us choose to worship God. The result is a plentiful harvest of joy, peace, and abundance. Others distance themselves from God by foolishly worshiping things of this earth such as fame, fortune, or personal gratification. To do so is a terrible mistake with eternal consequences.

How can we ensure that we cast our lot with God? We do so, in part, by the practice of regular worship in the company of fellow believers. When we worship God faithfully and fervently, we are blessed. When we fail to worship God, for whatever reason, we forfeit the spiritual gifts that He intends for us. Every day provides opportunities to put God where He belongs: at the center of our lives. When we do so, we worship not just with our words, but with deeds, and that's as it should be. For believers, God comes first. Always first.

God actually delights in and pursues our worship
(Proverbs 15:8 & John 4:23).

Shirley Dobson

The Joy of Worship

Praise Him! Praise Him!
Tell of His excellent greatness. Praise Him!
Praise Him! Ever in joyful song!

Fanny Crosby

Spiritual worship comes from our very core
and is fueled by an awesome reverence
and desire for God.

Beth Moore

Happy are those who hear the joyful call
to worship, for they will walk in the light
of your presence, LORD.

Psalm 89:15 NLT

Heavenly Father, let today and every day be
a time of worship. Let me worship You, not only
with words and deeds, but also with my heart.
In the quiet moments of the day, let me praise You
and thank You for creating me, loving me,
guiding me, and saving me.

~Amen